Drawing Robots

Learning to draw amazing unusual subjects

By Amy Hughes

Table of Contents

Disclaimer

While all attempts have been made to verify the information provided in this book, the author does assume any responsibility for errors, omissions, or contrary interpretations of the subject matter contained within. The information provided in this book is for educational and entertainment purposes only. The reader is responsible for his or her own actions and the author does not accept any responsibilities for any liabilities or damages, real or perceived, resulting from the use of this information.

The trademarks that are used are without any consent, and the publication of the trademark is without permission or backing by the trademark owner. All trademarks and brands within this book are for clarifying purposes only and are the owned by the owners themselves, not affiliated with this document.

Introduction

I want to thank you and congratulate you for downloading the book, "How to draw Robots".

This book contains proven steps and strategies on how to draw robots.

{Provide any additional information about the book. Make sure the introduction SELLS the book, as people can see this when they preview it on Amazon or Kindle}.

Here Is A Preview Of What You'll Learn...

- Subtle elements are vital in this third phase of robotic drawing advancement, and we can begin to add more outline elements to our robot plan, wires and different catches can be included and a clear robot face makes the robot show up without any feelings.

- Tidying the drawing up is a smart thought as well and inking over the pencil lines makes your drawing emerge.

- Drawing robots is something that can be learnt like whatever other thing you can figure out how to draw, so simply appreciate utilizing your creative energy to make them.

Much, much more!

Thanks again for downloading this book, I hope you enjoy it!

Chapter 1 – Robot 1

Robots by their exceptionally nature are sci-fi and this zone engages numerous aficionados of the class, thus it is very right that we experience another drawing article on the most proficient method to draw an advanced robot starting with no outside help, take note of that this article and the accompanying connection are just a thought of motivation and one conceivable approach to draw a robot as you possess creative energy will apply to your own particular robot manifestations.

The middle of the robot is similar to one vast fat oval egg shape that doesn't need to be focused over right now, insofar as it freely associate with the various robot parts, for example, the arms, legs and the head.

The above technique is perfect for drawing robots, particularly as you are stamping in every one of the regions that you need to characterize, however it essentially doesn't need to remain as such, not with it being a robot at any rate, there is a propensity to attempt and draw an excess of subtle element comfortable starting, yet this is prompted against as the more you figure out how to draw from the begin by arranging your representations then the better your drawings will be each time you draw.

The following step is to gradually transform them wieners and circles into genuine robot body parts that appear as though they would move and be vital working parts, to do this you can simply portray over the circle and barrel shapes by utilizing them as the first system, let your creative ability assume control right now, in light of the fact that you need to imagine a cutting edge robot with overwhelming metal plated covering, or something that takes after metal packaging, we could likewise outline in a weapon on one of the robot arms just to check whether it lives up to expectations.

Squares, rectangles and circles are expected to figure out how to draw a robot that does resemble a sensible machine! Undoubtedly, drawing a cartoon robot is a simple assignment on the off chance that you definitely know how to draw a couple of essential shapes. In any case, drawing a "cool" robot is more troublesome in the event that you don't have much involvement with cartoon characters. Utilizing this drawing lesson, I will demonstrate to you how apprentices can accomplish something extraordinary utilizing just a couple of straightforward methods. How about we begin now!

Robot 1:

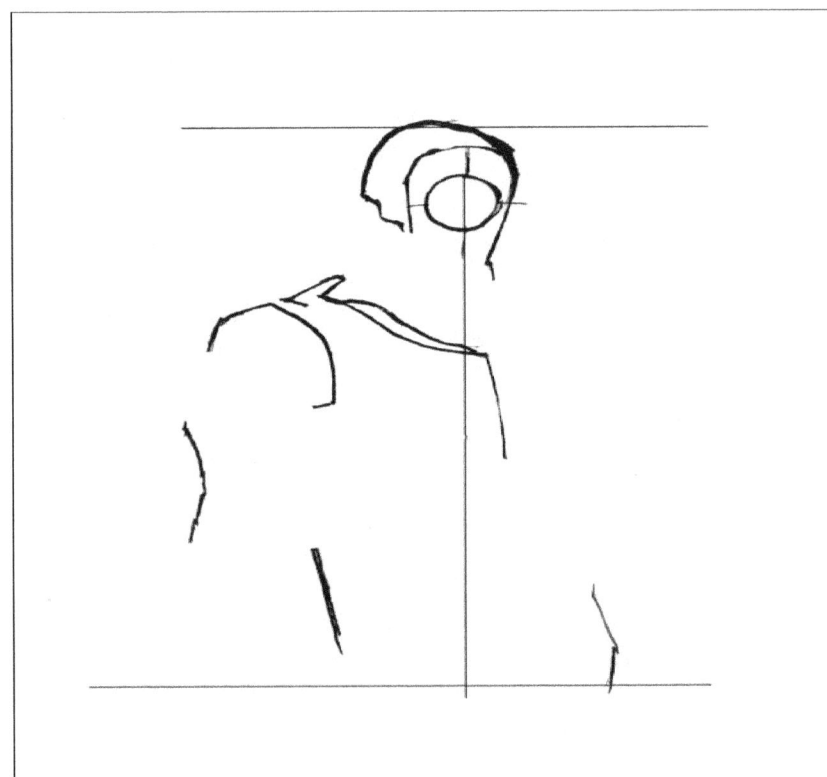

Step 1

Cool! We should start this drawing lesson with the formation of a huge oval shape to represent the head. Underneath the head, show some lines to show the body of robot. At long last, draw a few lines to represent the body.

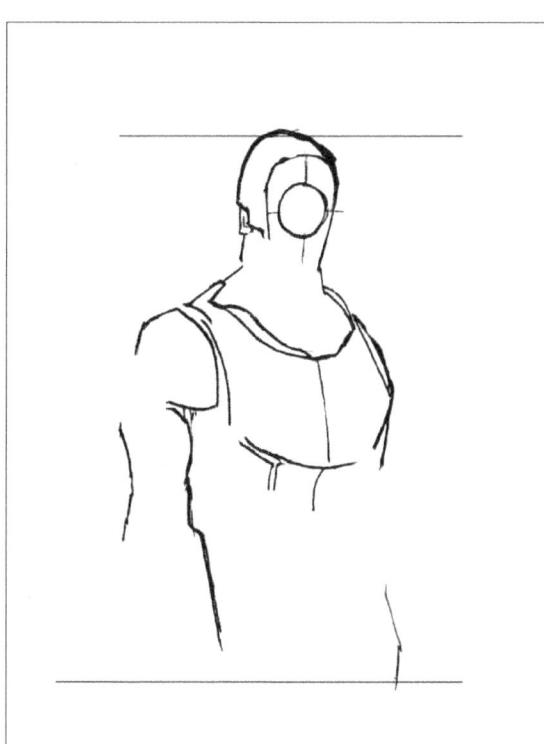

Step 2

Beneath the body, outline two little lines to show the body. See the representation above on the off chance that you require a picture to bail you make sense of how to make this some piece of the instructional exercise.

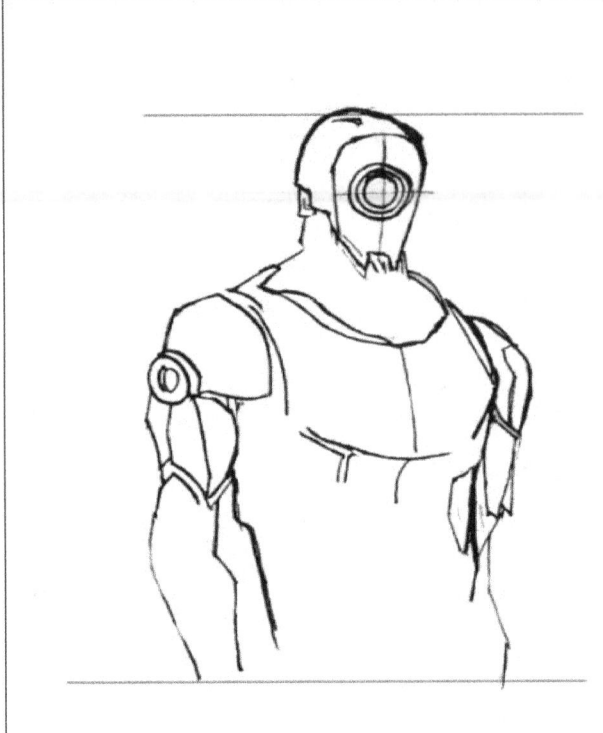

Step 3

On the leader of the robot, draw a little reception apparatus utilizing a meager rectangle and a little circle. The arms are made with since quite a while ago bended lines and the hands are made from little roundabout shapes with a missing piece (well, much the same as a pie with a cut missing may resemble). And to show the body we can use a few other lines and shapes.

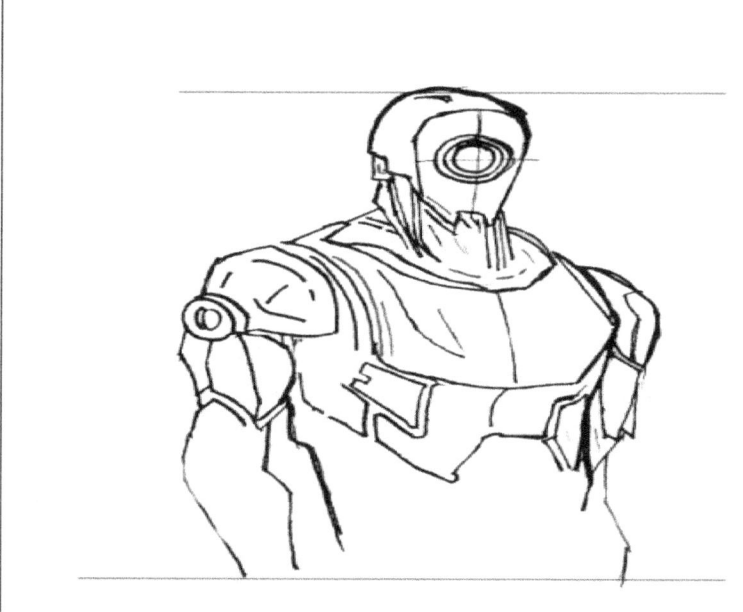

Step 4

Inside the body, you can include a few components like a few more unparallel lines as well as shapes just to describe the body of the robot. The eyes and the students are produced using vast roundabout shapes. The mouth is outlined with a sketching.

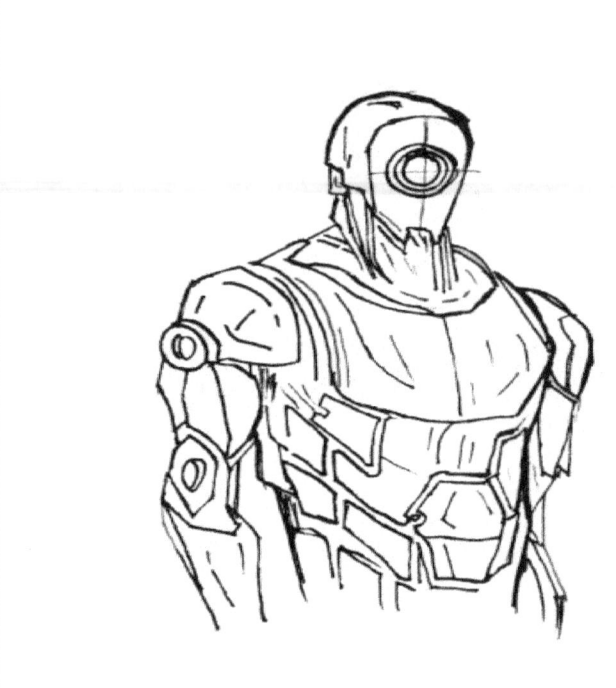

Step 5

Complete this adding so as to draw instructional exercise little oval shapes inside the understudies. You can likewise include more points of interest the body of the robot like demonstrated in the representation above.

This cartoon robot is without a doubt the most straightforward one to draw on this site. On the other hand, you can likewise attempt this charming adaptation produced using fundamental shapes as well, yet loaded with inclination hues and impacts.

On the off chance that you lean toward something all the more difficult, this robot offers everything you need to make a part of sketch representation utilizing a vector application.

Chapter 2 – Robot 2

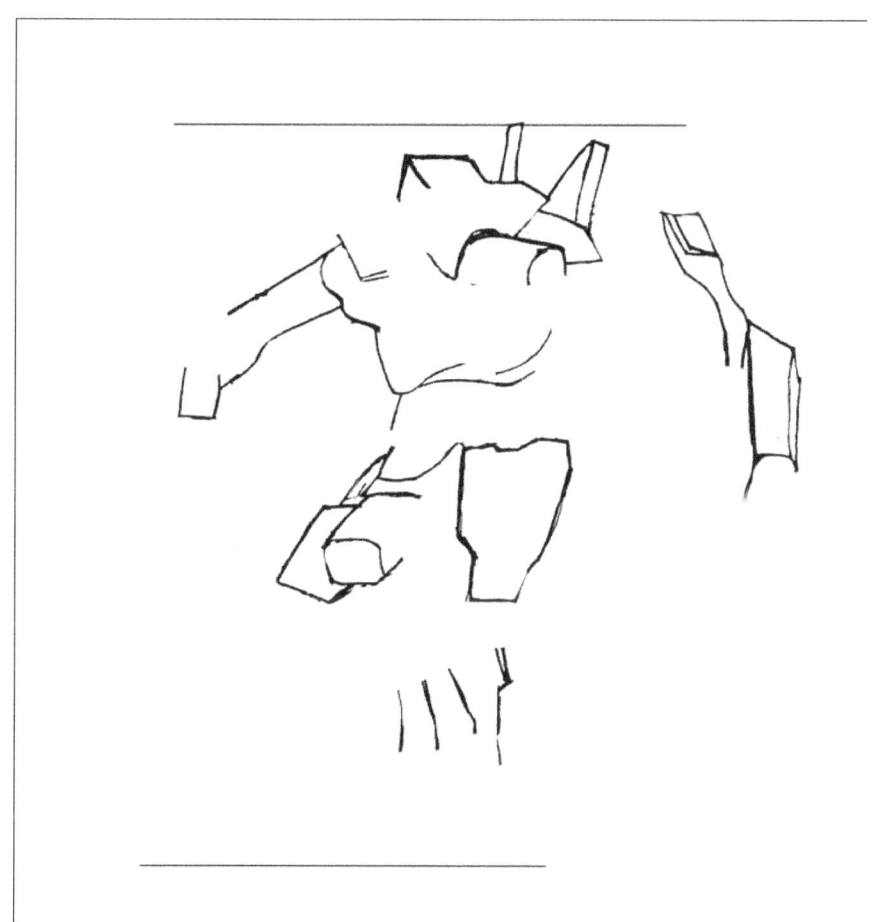

Step 1:

In order to make a figure like this, start with making 2 lines from where to start and where to end. And start with making lines for legs which will be completed later in the steps. And you can make the upper thighs for the robot and we can move towards the upper body. For the upper body of the robot sketch a few lines to show the chest and hands in parallel to it. After that you can make the upper part of the robot.

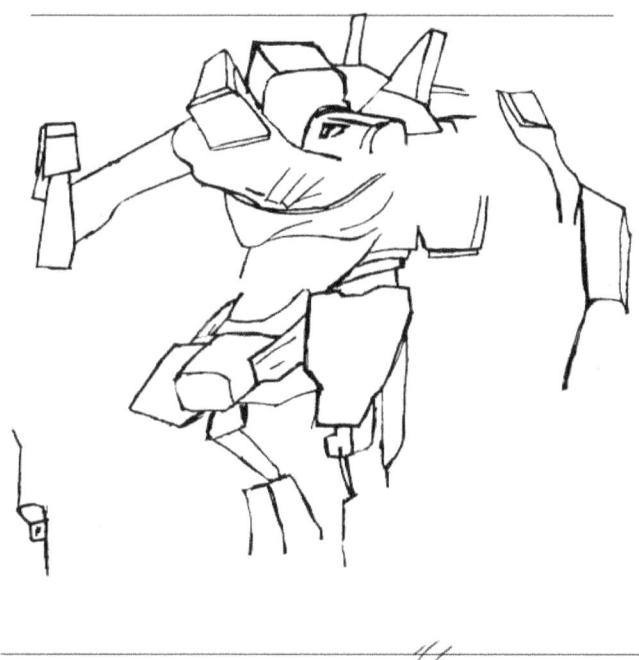

Step 2:

As we have now come to the second step of the robot we can start it by completing the legs as we have already made some lines. And with that to complete the robot we can start with the body as the chest area and clothes we have already outlined in the 1st step. And give it a look of a robot by sketching few more lines.

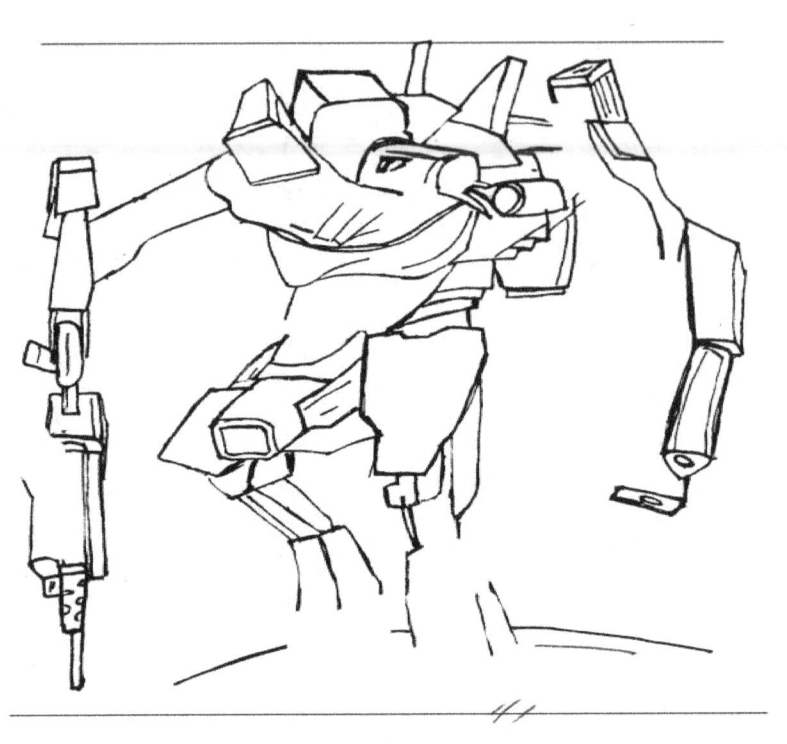

Step 3:

Now since the robot's body is coming to finishing up. We can make a gun or anything other if you want in his one hand. Now you can make the body better by sketching few parts of the robot.

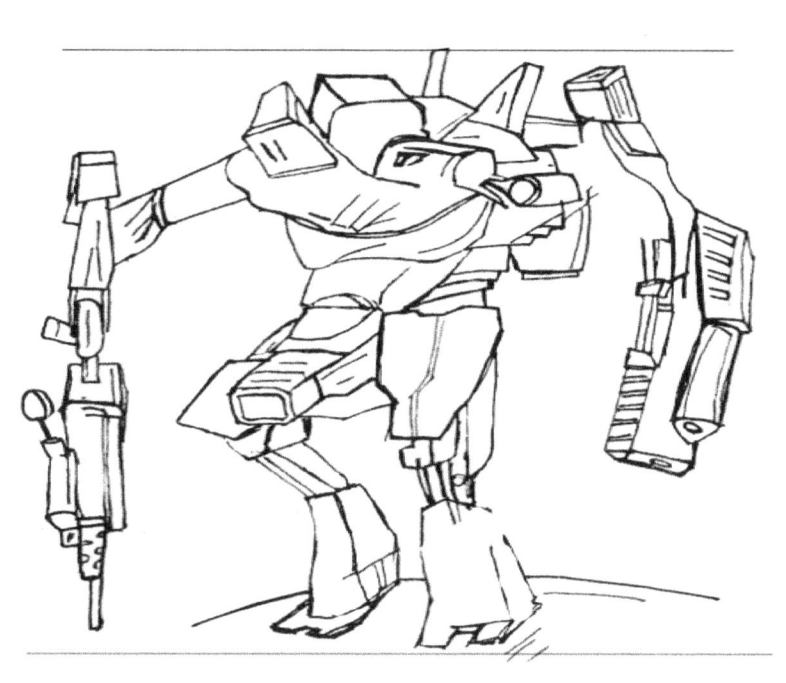

Step 4:

Now we have finished with the help of sketching and drawing parallel and unparallel lines and a few shapes.

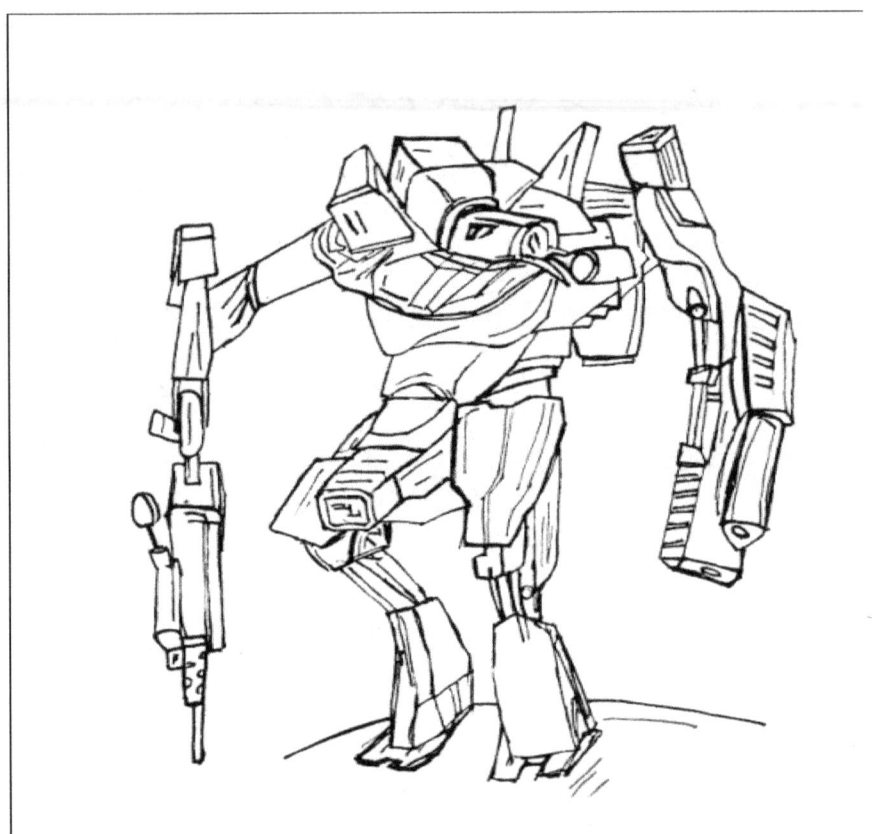

Step 5:

After erasing the lines which we made during the step 1st to show
the entire robot under that we can erase and sketch few parts of
the robot to make it look better.

Chapter 3 - Robot 3

Step 1:

Sketch the wireframe to speak to the robot's figure and represent (every circle speaks to a joint). And make a few lines so that we can join them all later on in other steps. And make a circle where we can show the face or a helmet later on.

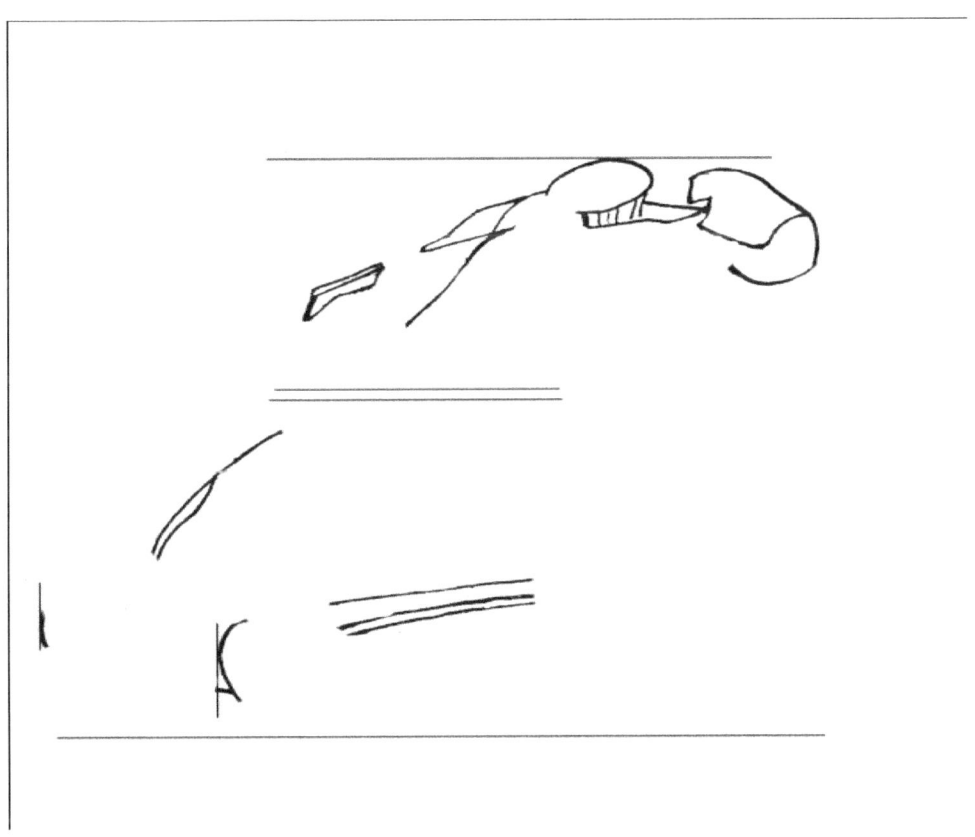

Step 2:

Use 3 dimensional shapes, for example, chambers, box shapes and circles to outline the body parts required. After that we can start with making upper side of the shoulder.

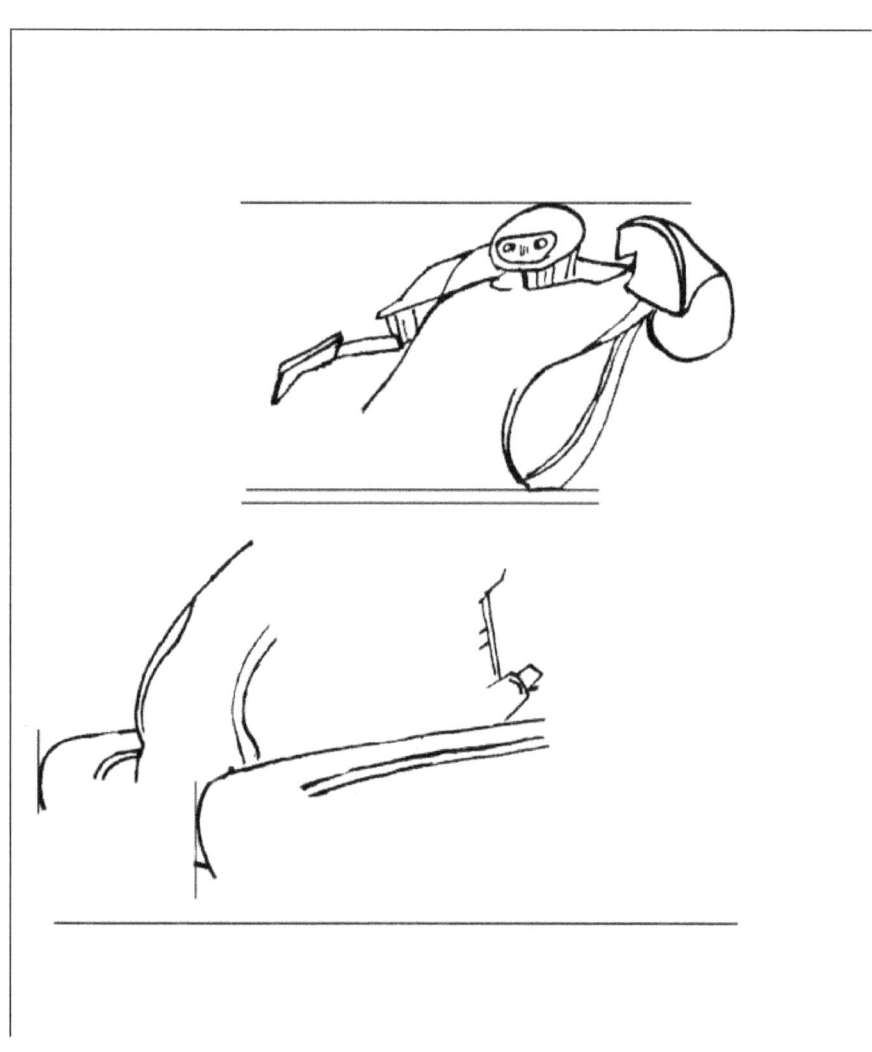

Step 3:

Use your imagination to draw robot highlights over the representation to make your own particular outline. By giving the legs a different shape here we tend to make a roller over there. So we can give that machine a different drawing in the same.

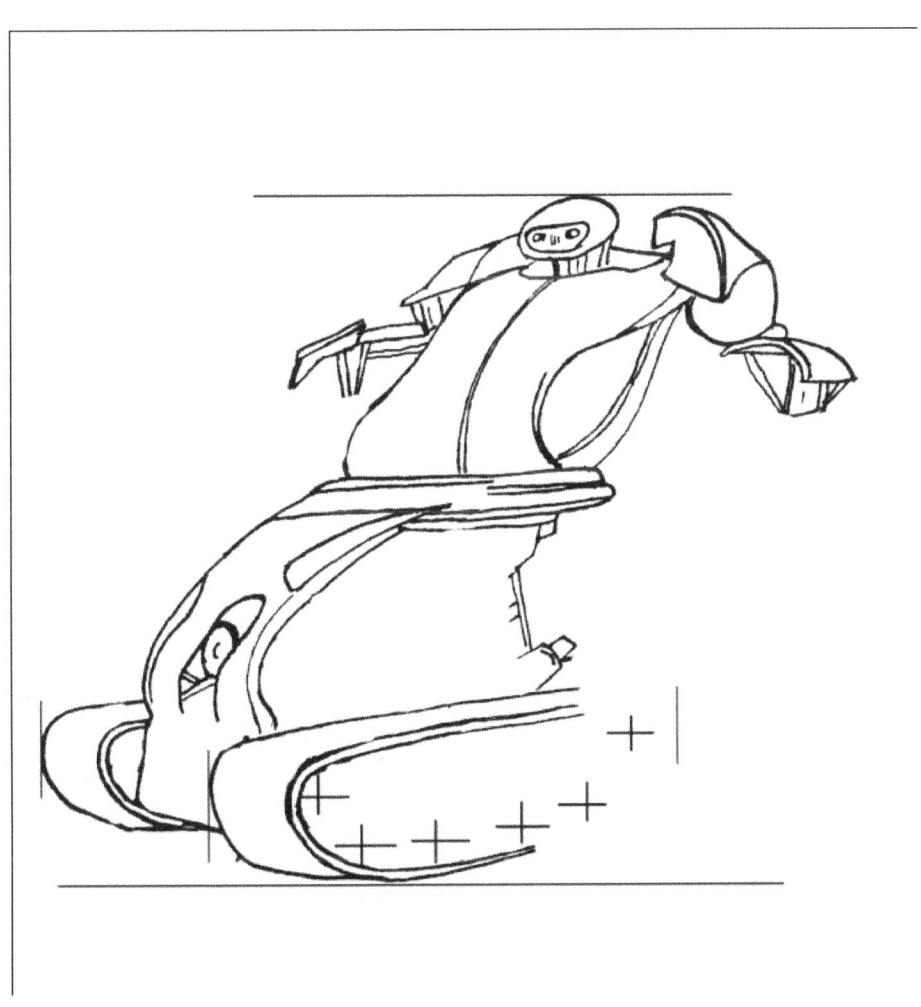

Step 4:

Refine the portrayal utilizing a littler tipped drawing device to include more detail. As we have added the face here with proper explanations such as eyes and mouth, by this we are trying to show that the robot is wearing a helmet.

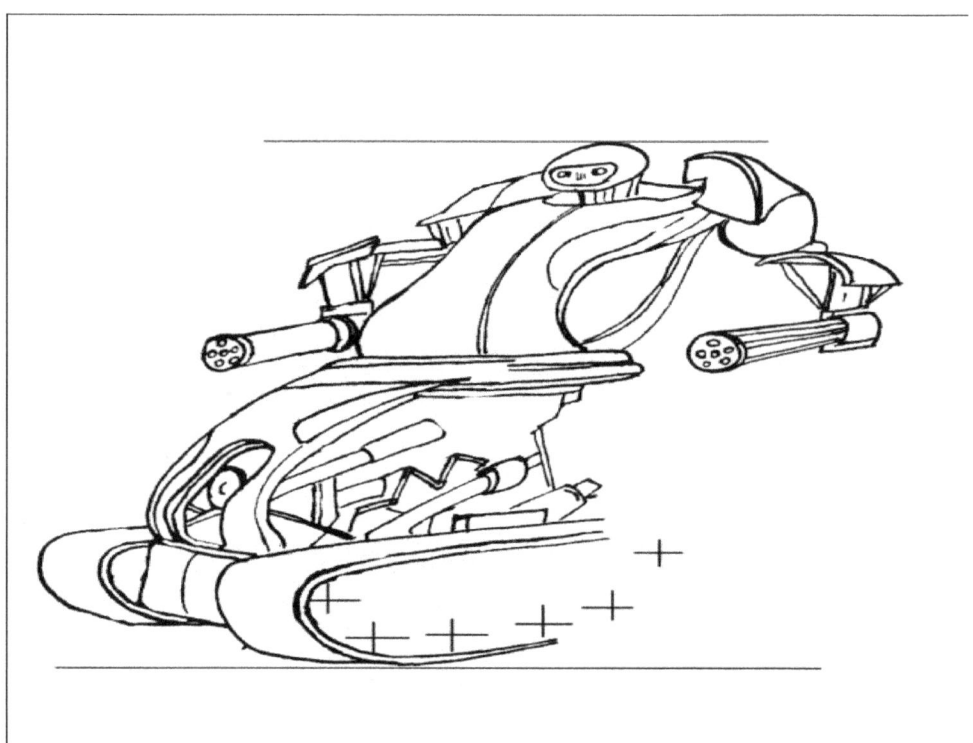

Step 5:

Erase and uproot representation lines to make clean laid out drawing. And sketch the part where the machine of roller is and give the hands a few guns by making long standing cylinders.

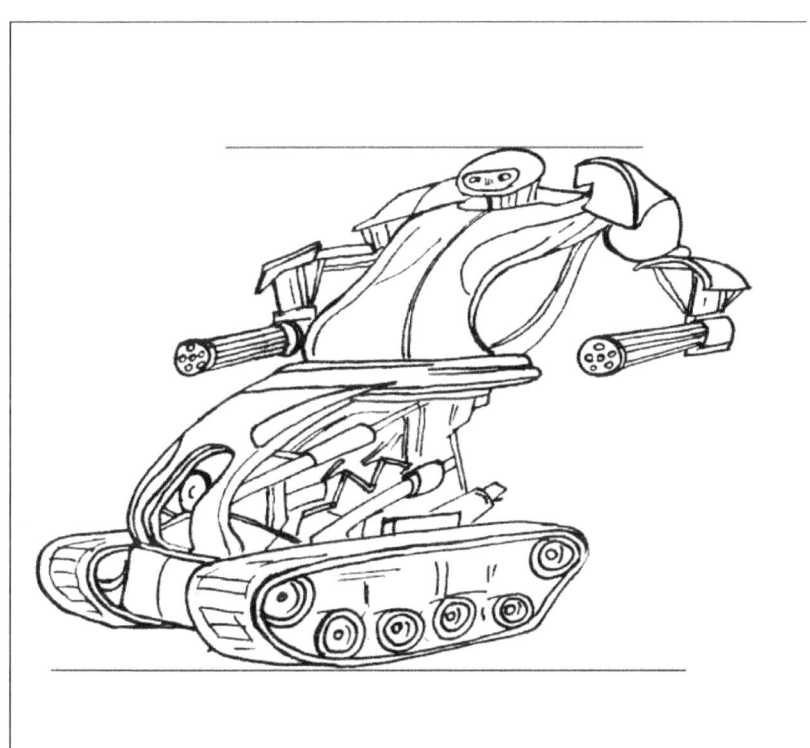

As you can see in the above image the robot has been completed with proper sketching where ever it was needed and we have completed the tires of the roller. So the robot looks complete and fine.

Chapter 4 - Robot 4

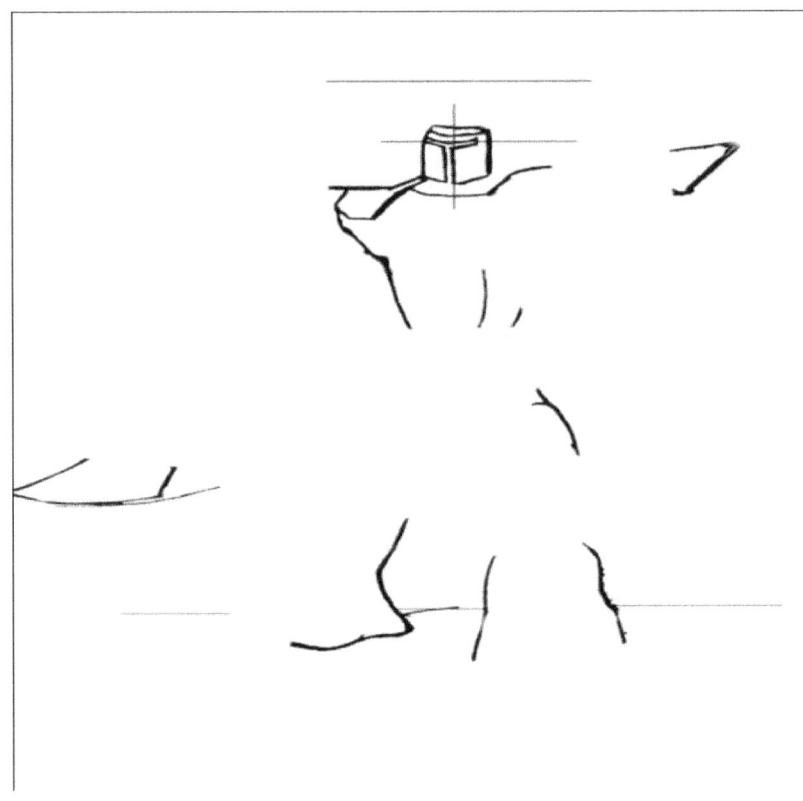

Step 1:

Design a robot utilizing various types of 3 dimensional shapes (diverse box shapes, chambers, wedges, etc...).

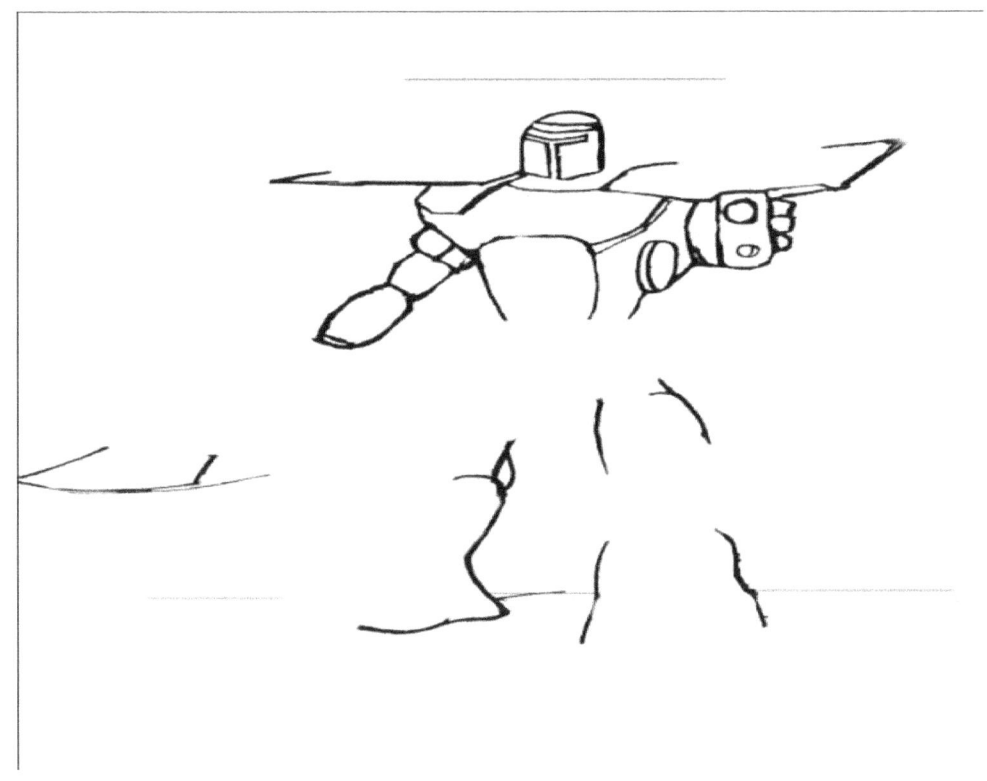

Step 2:

Sketch extra points of interest and parts like joints, hardware and apparatuses.

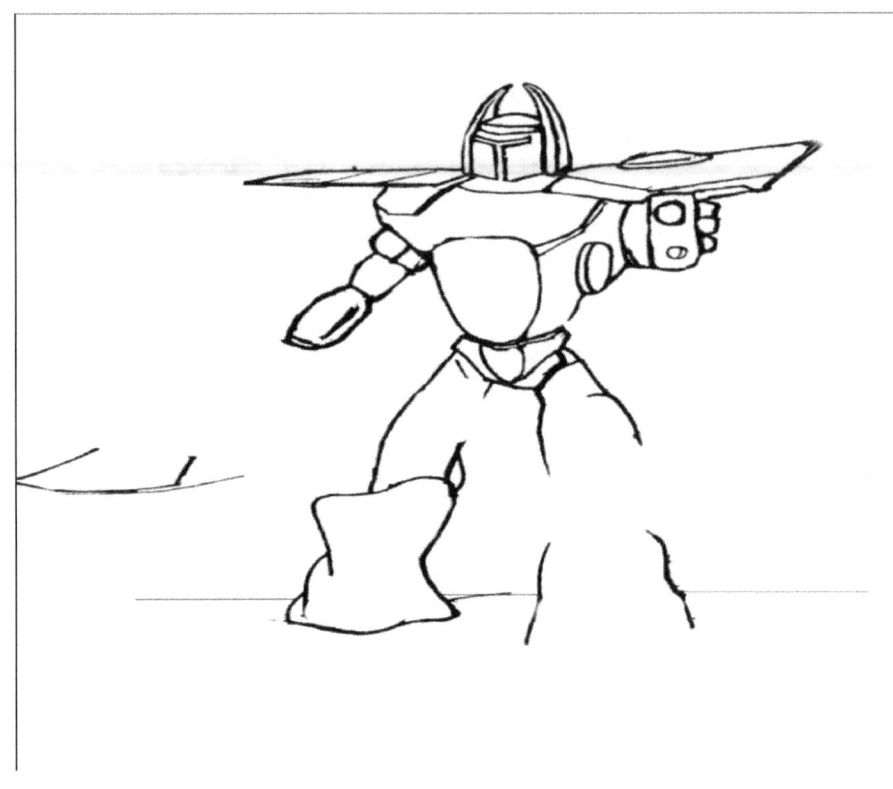

Step 3:

Refine the portrayal by utilizing a littler tipped drawing device.

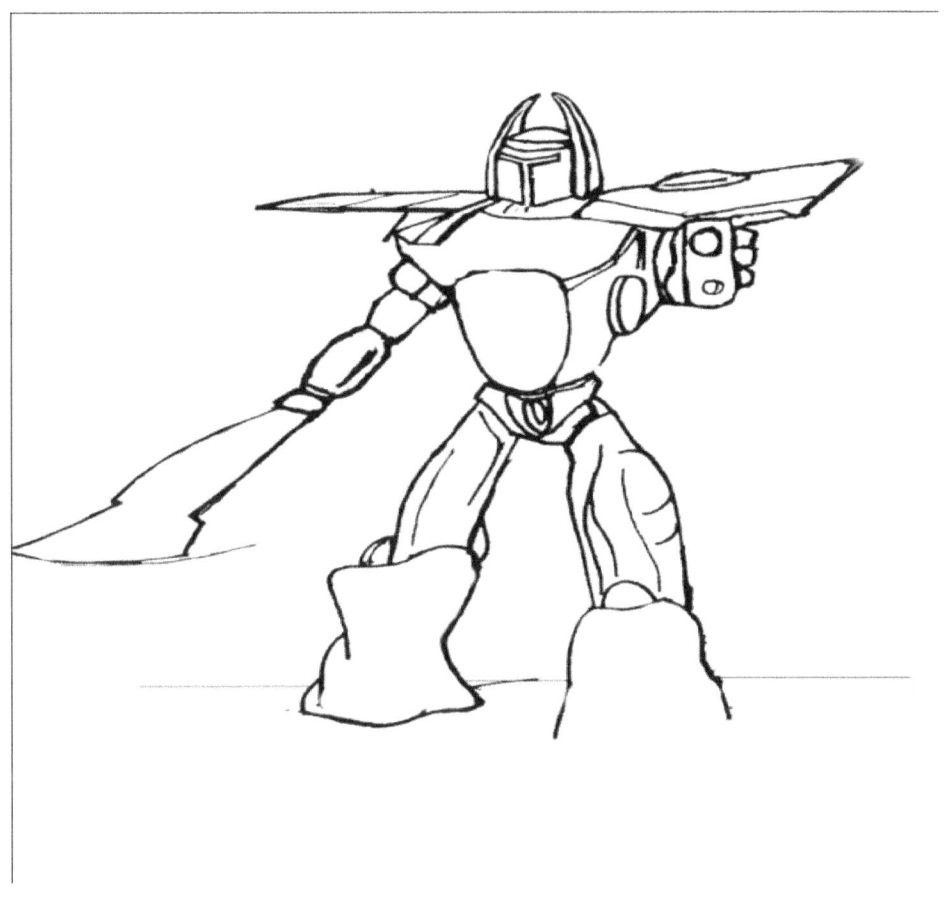

Step 4:

Create plots by drawing over the last portray.

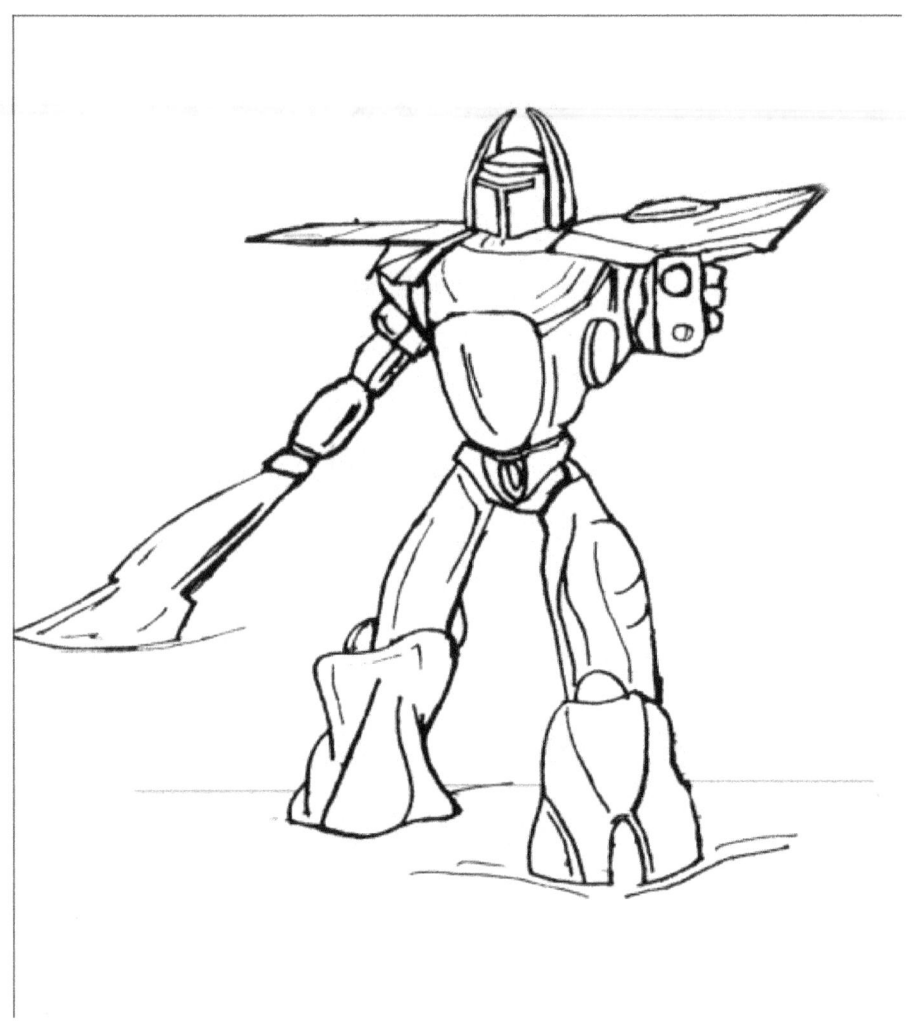

Step 5:

Erase and evacuate the portrayal lines to make a clean delineated drawing.

Chapter 5- Robot 5

Let's assume you need to construct a robot. What do you need to do? Presently, there are three fields or orders you must be acquainted with. There are the mechanical, gadgets and programming viewpoints. Less you think about these three, don't tackle a robotic venture. Today, we will discuss just on mechanical part of building a robot.

Each robot has a structure. Whether an unbending or adaptable structure (contingent upon your robot sort), you will need to plan it. How to outline, you inquire? All things considered, you can utilize routine portrayals like your pencil drawings on a bit of paper. On the other hand, professionally, outline these in "computer aided design" programs, regularly known as Computer Aided Software. What these product can accomplish for you is add to these portrayals you have made, into a more sensible looking one, in you're PC. On your screen, you will see your structure wake up as you roll out improvements, little or huge.

Numerous trials and lapses will be experienced when you utilize these "computer aided design" programming. Among numerous projects, I utilize the 'AutoDESK Inventor' for every one of my outlines. Of late, I have been included in my college last year venture.

The most critical thing is to begin some place. Draw something. Anything which you believe is conceivable to change over it to a moving workable robot. I have done it, and if you. In any case, recall, the first step is dependably the hardest. It is similar to playing the guitar. The beginning is constantly agonizing and moderate.

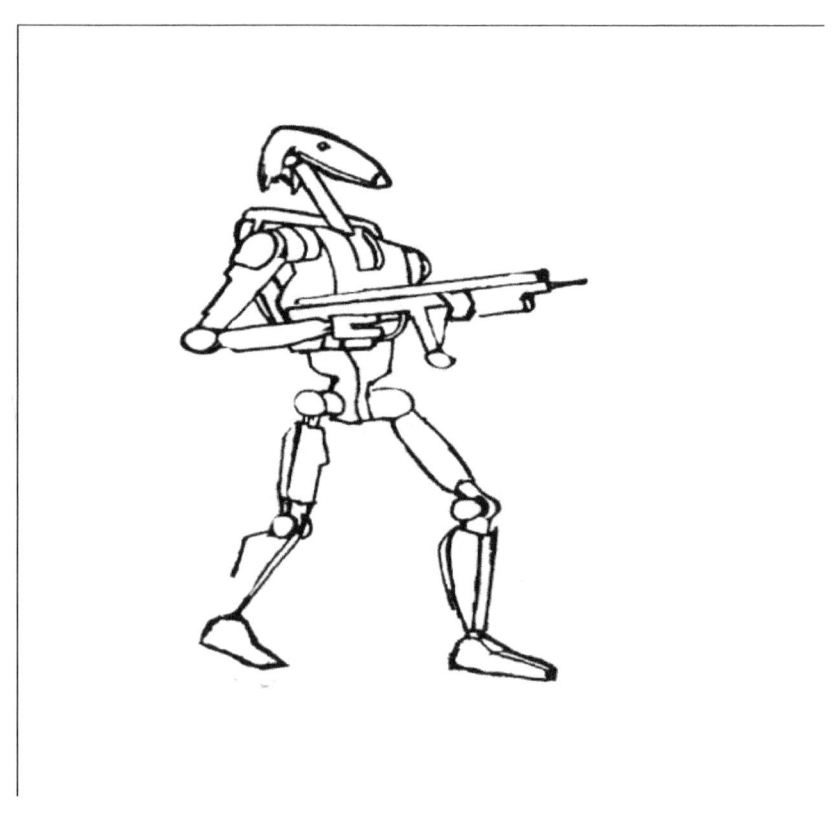

Step 1:

Draw speedy representations of robots. By utilizing outline drawing you can record your thoughts and choose what robot you need to draw. It could be a four legged robot, in view of a creature or a fight sort robot or only a basic family robot.

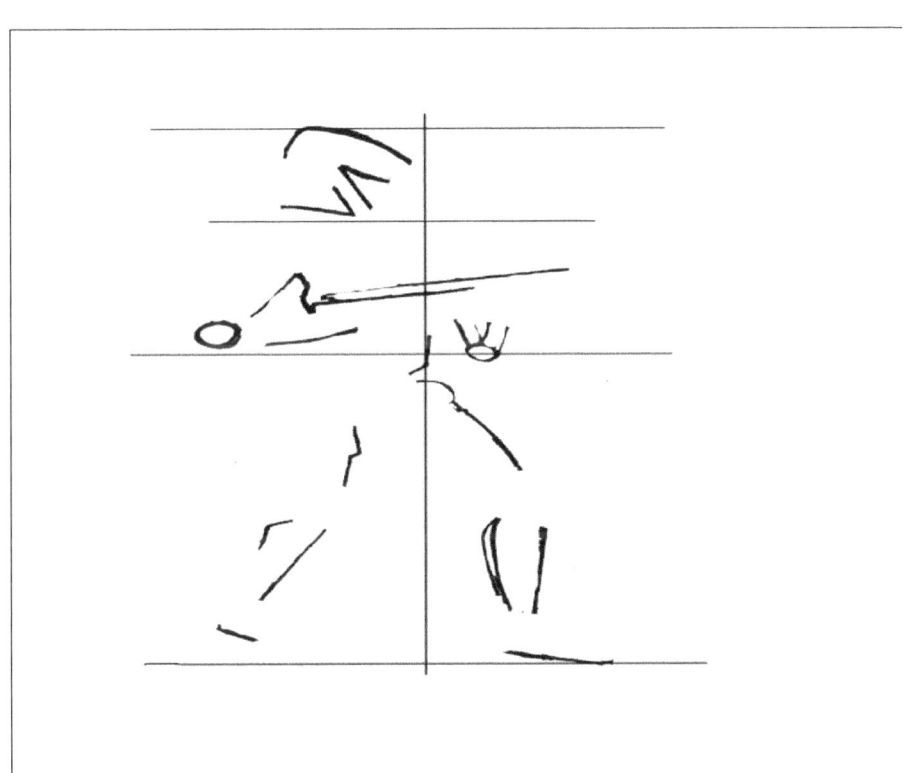

Step 2:

From your drawings, pick a configuration you like the most. You can likewise join a few components present in your different outlines.

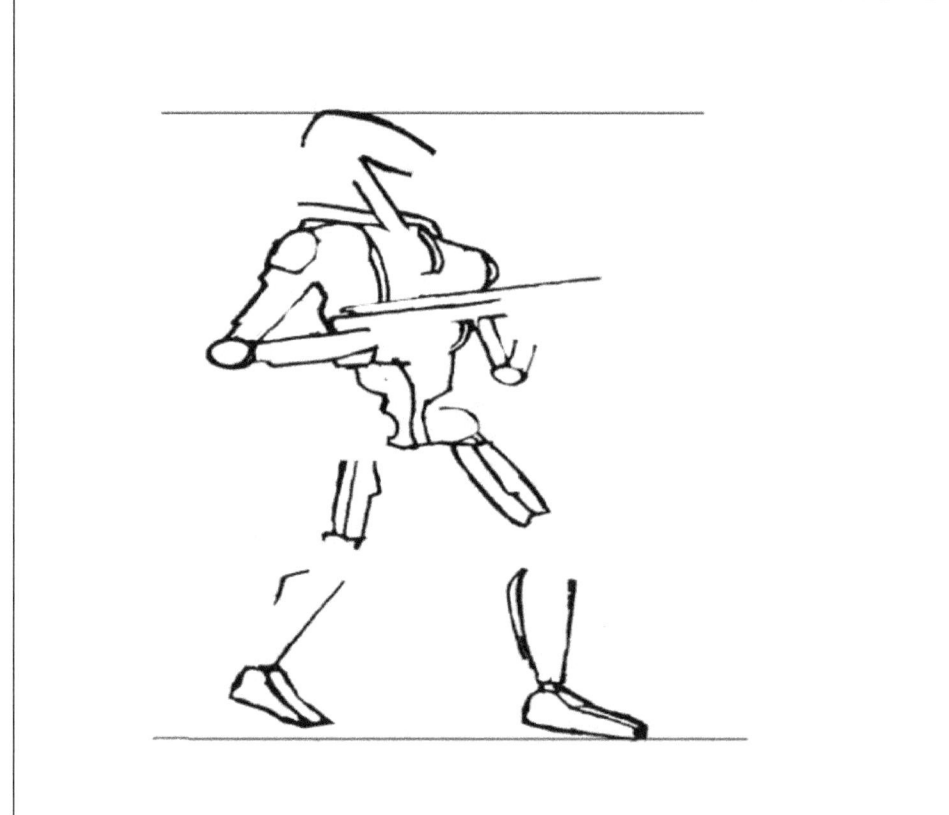

Step 3:

Draw your line craftsmanship. Begin with the fundamental shapes, make it straightforward and clear.

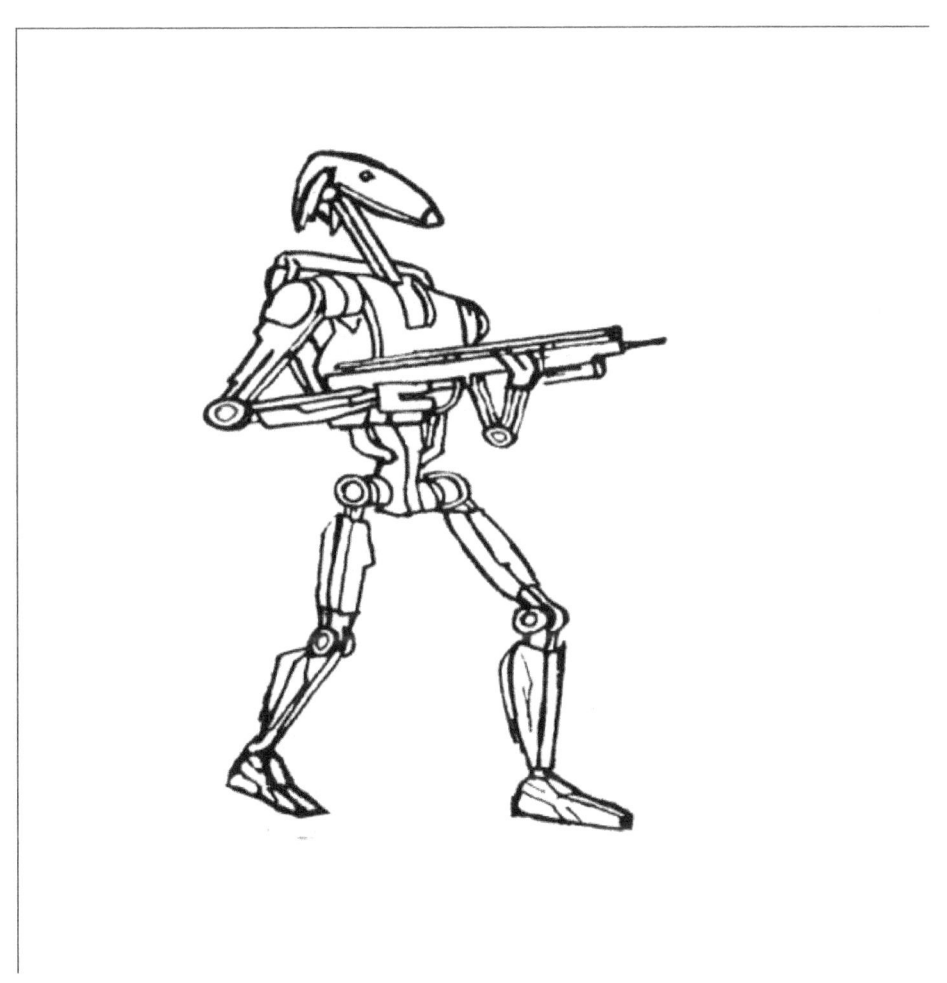

Step 4:

Erase your outline drawing and include better points of interest, similar to the wires, links, plan on the head and mid-section, and so on.

Conclusion

Subsequent to outsourcing for materials, generally one will begin building the robotic task structure. In this article, creation and development strategies and routines are talked about.

When you have at long last chosen your materials, be it steel or aluminum or wood or plastic cardboard, you can begin applying every one of your outlines, portrayed prior. I would recommend you layout the important parts on a hard cardboard first. At that point slice the cardboard to pieces that make your robot structure.

Test them out on these cardboard structures. In the event that conceivable, use clasp like stray pieces. Something else, utilizing epoxy or any significant cement arrangement will work. Build them. Utilization scissors and tapes to get those individual cut out parts connected. At that point make them as close as could be expected under the circumstances to the genuine structure (utilizing materials you have discovered or purchased). This is imperative in order to test out the configuration.

Odds are, there will be blunders or deformities. At that point, take this risk to enhance a superior configuration. Extemporization is the heart of any exchange. I can just guide you towards building robots. Not let you know what to do in moment points of interest. Show a man how to catch a fish, and you will help him out in life, rather than giving him the fish.

Check whether there are any deformities of geometrical obliges or blunders. On the off chance that your arranging or configuration had been great, the structure ought to turn out fine. Something else, update or do a conceptualize via hunting on the Internet down outline thoughts. Investigate other created (items as of now in the business sector), particularly.

When you have an effective model produced using these cardboard, then the time has come to exchange it to the genuine materials you have acquired and outsourced with so much exertion (and perhaps cash).

At the point when finding out about robots, a great many people consider Robocop or The Iron Man, that is for the most part about characters from acclaimed books and TV shows. What's more, that is on the grounds that in the vast majority's brains robots must look to some extent like man and his physiognomy. Be that as it may, despite the fact that both the first portrays of robots and the first creations of the procedure, had a human-like appeal, these days the greater part of the robots just take from man his physical capacities which, with the assistance of the most recent disclosures, are taken to the most astounding level of flawlessness. Most robots are truth be told electrical circuits blessed with exact capacities exceptionally planned by man.

In old times there were slaves and creatures that did the challenging assignments favored men discovered either messy or humble, so that they could manage issues that were quite vital. What's more, that is the manner by which the first robots were conceived. As progress and innovation developed, man's yearning to fabricate a human-like system that could help and bolster him worked out as expected. The main complex machines were considered to perform redundant errands, additionally exercises difficult to achieve by a person in view of his impediments. Along these lines robots turned into every capable machine that enhanced man's life.

It is verging on difficult to envision today's existence without the assistance of robots or separate one from another. Clothes washers, autos, number crunchers, threshers or vacuum cleaners, robots have gotten to be crucial. What's more, this is particularly found in those areas where man can't perform the same undertakings in view of his constraints. In solution, for instance, robots are utilized to keep and procedure synthetic examples or even to perform greatly meticulous operations, in the armed force to show signs of improvement exactness or to have an impervious cautious framework, in developments to quicken and render conceivable the building of forcing structures.

The advancement made in pharmaceutical until today is mostly because of robots as well. While man works with information to make new pharmaceutical items that can mend even the most serious sicknesses, robots help them save the information and work it in a suitable way. They make the ideal atmosphere for synthetic examples to be put away in, they work the massive database of substances, stock and oversee it or perform certain operations that oblige unbounded accuracy. It is upon their intercession that human experts venture in and proceed with their exploration.

In any case, there are additionally the individuals who contend that robots are innovations that prompt estrangement and even devastation. The greater parts of them allude to disastrous occasions ever, whose achievement has just been conceivable with the assistance of robots. What they have a tendency to overlook is that all things considered, robots are just omnipotent hands, worked by a cerebrum, which fits in with individuals.

Illustrators should have the capacity to draw harsh representations of pretty much everything. They never recognize what their next task will be. Recently, we have seen a wide range of intriguing new things appear in liveliness; techno-transformable robots, unmanned airborne vehicles, and outsider shuttle. If you somehow managed to request that an artist draw something like this, they need to utilize their inventiveness and creative energy and after that consolidate it with their CAD/CAM programming PC abilities. This is a great deal simpler said than done.

Everybody eventually persuades the inclination to be imaginative. Numerous individuals are magnificently gifted; their office for innovative believed is much formed and makes an interpretation of effortlessly energetically. Obviously the dominant part of us is only stayed with the innovative inclination and no real way to effortlessly express it.

Are these two sorts of individuals distinctive? Not in any way. They are both individuals with trusts dreams and thoughts. What has the effect? Why are a few individuals great at communicating in their specialty and others not?

It's a close apostasy to say it however I believe it's anything but difficult to turn into an imaginative virtuoso in the event that you know the mystery. It comes down to this:

Having the desire to do something

Having the ability and experience to execute it

Stage One: Having the Urge

THE ART OF COMPOSITION

Inventive urges travel every which way however it's just workmanship in the event that you complete it. Whether it be visual craftsmanship like painting, comic books, model or film, or sound like music or talked word, or composing for books or screenplays, it just truly gets to be workmanship on the off chance that you arrange it, execute it and discharge it for the thought of your group of onlookers. Up to that point anything you create is practice.

The procedure of creation is called synthesis, and it's the way you get from your essential uncut precious stone of a thought to a cleaned and finished piece, and you'll discover this is an unmistakable procedure in any order.

You begin from a thought, generally simply the one. A scene, a picture, a sound or even an odor can be the motivation. It doesn't make a difference. The fact of the matter arrives is a beginning stage, something which energizes you. By then it just speaks to you as a result of some individual peculiarity of cerebrum science you can appreciate the entire thought just from that one flash of unique thought. You rationally fill in the spaces yourself and skirt points of interest and appreciate the thought about the completed workmanship.

Narrating is similar to spellbinding, a delicate, measured, pleasingly tweaked voice letting you know things in a precisely organized request to get a particular reaction from you. It doesn't the spell till you are prepared to get the recommendation (to stop smoking or whatever) then it drives you delicately over into cognizance and liking the experience. Your group of onlookers ought to feel that about your written work or other workmanship, better for the experience. Be that as it may, it's the same procedure, you tenderly lead individuals in, recount to them a story, then delicately push them to the way out ideally with a warm shine. So...

Step 1: MAKE LOTS OF LITTLE IDEAS

Portrayals, pictures off the web, notes on record cards, perfect Moleskine scratch pad brimming with those things and substantially more. It doesn't make a difference. Gather your thoughts in an unmistakable structure. The reason you have to have more than one thought is that thoughts group together and they have a weight, similar to a sort of imaginative mass. The cerebrum cherishes mixes of thoughts, and spaces between the thoughts. Huh? Spaces? Yes, the unfilled spaces between thoughts are as imperative as the thoughts. It's called juxtaposition. The mind sees 2-3 pictures and tries to join them. You can't help it. A photo of a wolf, a kid and a sheep give you one thought; a photo of a wolf, a young lady and the moon gives you another very surprising thought.

So from these thoughts take a couple to frame the center of your piece, the topic, the song or the shape.

Step 2: CHOOSE YOUR CORE

Having sorted through the thoughts you pick the key things which speak to you the center of what you need to say... What, you don't have anything to say? Well this reasons you an issue. Craftsmanship speaks the truth saying something. Presently don't get frightened. It doesn't need to be a significant thought, yet it has to be an idea, and it must be your idea.

Step 3: CHOOSE A STYLE

As a craftsman with years of experience you will obviously have the capacity to approach any number of styles to put your thoughts over. Alright perhaps not. In the event that you are that skilled I'm extremely satisfied for you. In any case, the majority of us need to strive to locate a suitable style which we can possess.

A preventative note here: I'm not saying that you abstain from delivering anything till you have developed your own unique style. THe best approach to advance an individual style is to get the hang of what you do and realizing from existing styles is a vital piece of taking in your own style. That and practice. When you have a great deal of work added to your repertoire you can take a style and make it you're possess. Try not to stress over being unique at to begin with, simply attempt to take a style and utilization it to make your specialty. It may not be totally unique at first. Be that as it may, the more you work amid the cleaning stage, the more unique it will get to be. It may not begin that way but rather you can make it you're possess.

Presently then, how would you envision your work in a mixture of styles? Numerous individuals skirt this stride and begin in with the composition or drawing immediately, yet this is the most vital stride before any work can happen. Also, this is it: Considering

Yes genuinely, please permit yourself time to utilize your cerebrum in the way it jumps at the chance to be utilized. A decent methodology and one which lives up to expectations for me is a sort of guided reflection or self-entrancing schedule.

Locate a peaceful spot where you are not going to be irritated for 60 minutes. Get a clock or something to that affect which informs you with a tender ringer sound, similar to an alert on a mobile phone. Set it for 60 minutes. Unwind. Close your eyes. Take 20 profound, associated breaths. Feel yourself unwinding more profound and more profound with every breath. Consider your story, your piece, your film. Consider your thought and let your cerebrum wear down it like a billion small nano-robots, looking for the genuine state of the story. Delete anything which is not a piece of the shape. Sit the entire hour. On the off chance that you get another thought or nosy other thought which you have to record, have a pen and paper convenient so you can scribble it down to get it insane until later on. Vacant your brain and let the thought relax. At the point when the hour is up, animate yourself gradually and appreciate the mental opportunity which these sessions will give you.

Contemplations like this are unbelievably helpful for sharpening thoughts or giving them a chance to come to fruition. There is an inclination to attempt and power thoughts out in caffeine fuelled meetings to generate new ideas. Try not to do that. Try not to constrain it; let it out.

The human mind is an AMAZINGLY unpredictable and splendid machine and it will discover sense in any arbitrary occasions. So give it a chance to take a shot at your thoughts, your fundamental components of story or structure. Utilize the spellbinding or contemplation procedures I've portrayed to free up your cerebrum's imaginative squeezes and permit your thoughts to develop and come to fruition. (These are effective methods which I want to utilize and I'll discuss them once more.)

When you have a couple crisply developed thoughts and they are beginning to have a positive structure, you require a legitimate structure.

Step 4: BUILD A STRUCTURE FITTING THE SCOPE

In all workmanship there is a convention of building a hidden structure. In movement they make wire armatures to hang the mud on, in model as well. In painting there is the beginning charcoal drawings.

Structure is essential in light of the fact that you hang your current thoughts on it and afterward you see the space between them. You see what you haven't done yet and once you realize that you can begin putting in stuff in the spaces.